The Nest was conceived, edited and designed by
Frances Lincoln Limited, Apollo Works,
5 Charlton Kings Road, London NW5 2SB

WINDWARD
an imprint owned by W. H. Smith and Son Limited
Registered No. 237811, England
Trading as WHS Distributors
St. John's House, East Street, Leicester LE1 6NE

ISBN 0-7112-0530-2 paperback
ISBN 0-7112-0534-5 hardback

9 8 7 6 5 4 3 2 1

Printed and bound in Italy

Design and art direction   Debbie MacKinnon

The Nest

Chris Baines
& Penny Ives

FRANCES LINCOLN
WINDWARD

It's early in the Spring and time for the birds to find a place to build their nests. The black cock bird is looking in the old boot, while the brown hen bird looks under an old drink-can. But these places on the ground wouldn't be very safe for a nest.

That's better! The cock bird sings at the top of his voice, at the top of the apple tree. He wants everybody to know this is his new home.
His mate sits quietly amongst the branches. She is watching for signs of danger.

This is a safe place to build a nest, high up in the branches of the tree. But the top of the tree can be very shaky when the wind blows. The clever birds use their beaks to weave strong grasses in and out, backwards and forwards and round and round. The wind won't shake *this* nest loose. It's tightly tied to the twigs at the top of the tree.

Grass, moss, leaves! The birds look very funny – they're gathering all kinds of soft bits and pieces in their beaks. But birds don't eat things like this. Whatever can they be for?

So that's it! The nest is very strong on the outside, but lovely and soft on the inside. The hen bird has laid one shiny egg. The soft moss, grass and leaves are perfect for keeping the egg warm and safe.

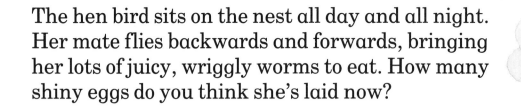

The hen bird sits on the nest all day and all night. Her mate flies backwards and forwards, bringing her lots of juicy, wriggly worms to eat. How many shiny eggs do you think she's laid now?

One! Two! Three! Four! The busy birds have
kept their four shiny eggs safe and warm
for days and days. Now they have hatched.
Four wide open mouths, in four wobbly
pink heads, on four wrinkly baby-bird bodies.
All they do, all day, is cheep-cheep-cheep!
– and then gobble up a grub – then
cheep-cheep-cheep! again for more food.

The baby birds need to eat lots
of squidgy green grubs every day.
Grubs make baby birds grow big and strong.
The parent birds are so busy hunting for food
that at first they don't notice the children
and their kitten.

Help! The parent birds are very frightened now.
They squawk at the kitten. They squawk at the
children. Please go away!
The baby birds are getting very hungry.
Cheep-cheep-cheep! More food please!
Cheep-cheep-cheep!
What if the kitten hears them?

The kitten has climbed up the tree – but after days and days of gobbling up grubs, and cheep-cheep-cheeping for food, the baby birds have grown feathers. Now they're big enough to fly.

As the parent birds flap their wings and squawk at the kitten, the four baby birds jump out of the nest and escape – just in time!